1756-1791

MOZART

1756-1791

MOZART

SMITHMARK

© 1995 Bookman International bv
Houtweg 11, 1251 CR Laren (NH)
The Netherlands

For this present English language edition: Todtri Productions, Ltd.,
New York

Text: Jeroen Koolbergen
Translation: Van Splunteren/Burret
Lay-out: ADM, Pieter van Delft

This edition published in 1996 by SMITHMARK Publishers, a divi-
sion of U.S. Media Holdings, Inc., 16 East 32nd Street, New York,
NY 10016

SMITHMARK books are available for bulk purchase for sales pro-
motion and premium use. For details write or call the manager of
special sales, SMITHMARK Publishers, 16 East 32nd Street, New
York, NY 10016; (212) 532-6600.

Printed and bound in Italy

ISBN 0-8317-3640-2

Introduction

Salzburg is the birthplace of Wolfgang Amadeus Mozart in the 18th century. The old inner city is bounded by the river Salzach. The landscape is dominated by two steep hills, the Kapuzinerberg on the right bank of the river and the Mönchberg on the left. On the Mönchberg stands the great edifice which was the residence of the archbishop, a powerful man whom the princes of the Habsburg Empire had to reckon with.

At the time of Mozart's birth the archbishop was Sigismund von Schrattenbach, a man of enormous religious and secular power – he was prince, high priest, primate of Germany, and the head of the Bavarian bishops. In 1772, he was succeeded by Hieronymus von Colloredo, an authoritarian with whom Mozart, a man of independent character, would later come into conflict. The provincial city of Salzburg profited greatly from the affluence of Bavaria and its economic and cultural capital, Munich. It was the strategic center of important trade routes and situated in an area where agriculture flourished and salt and precious metals were mined. The cultural life of the city was also determined by the archbishop, who maintained his own chapel for which Mozart's father, Leopold, wrote the music.

Wolfgang Amadeus could certainly have come into the world in less favorable circumstances. Nonetheless, the provincial atmosphere of Salzburg stifled him and eventually he would exchange the city of his birth for the much more cosmopolitan city of Vienna, just as Beethoven would do after him.

Mozart's life was well-documented by contempories, in words and in images, and in his own letters and those of his father. These will form the background to our journeys through Europe with the greatest musical child prodigy that has ever lived. And we will follow the life of the adult composer who by the time he died at the age of 35 had composed a huge and varied body of work, an oeuvre which continues to delight the world.

Mozart's first composition, Minuet and Trio for harpsichord in G major, K 1, *written when he was seven years old.*

Johannes Chrysostomus Wolfgangus Theophilus Mozart was born in a house on Getreidegasse in Salzburg at eight o'clock on the evening of January 27, 1756. He was the youngest child of Leopold Mozart and Anna Maria Pertl. His last Christian name, Theophilus, was soon changed to Amadeus, which means exactly the same ("loved by God"). Leopold was a violinist and composer in the service of the Archbishop of Salzburg, Sigismund von Schrattenbach, and had originally come from the Bavarian city of Augsberg. He entered the archbishop's service in 1743 and married in 1747. Of the seven children of the marriage, only two were still alive – Maria Anna Walburga Ignatia (1751–1829), whose pet name was "Nannerl," and Wolfgang Amadeus. The children received music lessons from their father as early as possible, and he noted their progress in his manuscript notebook. Mozart's earliest composition is also found there – his *Minuet and Trio for harp-*

The Salzburg of Mozart's youth. The palace of the archbishops is left on the Mönchberg. (Vienna, Museen der Stadt)

sichord in G minor, K I (Köchels Catalogue). This dates from 1763, when Mozart was seven years old. Leopold was a good father and a good teacher, but he kept a very tight rein on his children. He believed that music should be at the service of the Church and the aristocracy. This servitude also had its practical aspect – his livelihood depended on it.

Leopold was very proud of his two child prodigies. He decided to go on tour with them in order to supplement his income. The first journey, by boat along the Danube to Vienna, began on September 18, 1762. The Mozarts disembarked at various places on the way, including Passau, Linz, Mauthausen, and Stein in the

hope of giving concerts for the local nobility. Wolfgang, the youngest and most gifted, continually stole the show, although Nannerl also played the harpsichord extremely well.

Leopold Mozart, composer and violinist, in an etching by Jacob Andreas Friedrich. (Vienna, Museen der Stadt)

Wolfgang, six years old, in the court dress presented to him by Empress Maria Theresa of Austria. The painting probably was by the northern Italian artist, Pietro Antonio Lorenzoni, who painted it in Salzburg.

In October, in the Schönbrunn Palace in Vienna, they performed for members of the Imperial family, who were amazed at the Mozart family's talent for improvisation. As a token of her gratitude Empress Maria Theresa presented Wolfgang and Nannerl with court dress belonging to her own children. The Viennese aristocracy invited the young Mozarts everywhere – but Wolfgang caught scarlet fever and the string

of performances came to an end. On December 31, 1762, after Wolfgang had recovered, they set out on the return journey to Salzburg.

At home an unpleasant surprise was awaiting Leopold. The archbishop had not appointed him Kapellmeister (director of the court orchestra), as he had expected, but vice–Kapellmeister, a position he would retain until his death.

The Long Journey by Stagecoach.
(Vienna, Museen der Stadt)

Back in Salzburg, six–year–old Wolfgang now concentrated on the violin, an instrument to which, like the harpsichord, he turned his hand extremely well. In his position as vice–Kapellmeister his father did not have a great deal to do and received permission from the archbishop to take his children traveling again. Their tour through Europe lasted for three years and this time mother Anna Maria went, too. In June 1763, the whole family left for Munich. During a stop in Wasserburg Wolfgang demonstrated a new aspect of his talent. He was actually too small to play the organ sitting because his feet could not reach the pedals. His solution was to operate the pedals by standing on them – he was just tall enough to reach the manuals with his hands.

There were no fixed concert engagements during the tour. Everything was left to chance and on their travels they often came across fellow–musicians undertaking similar journeys. In Munich the Mozarts were received at the Nymphenburg Palace by Prince Maximilian III, Elector of Bavaria. Here Mozart gave a display of his newly–acquired mastery of the violin and in so doing earned 100 florins. At another concert, Duke Clemens of Bavaria rewarded him with 65 florins.

The successes in Munich also showed clearly the difference between the two child prodigies. Nannerl was indeed a virtuoso on the harpsichord but she could not compose, while Wolfgang was astounding listeners with his first

compositions. We know from Leopold's letters that Nannerl was sometimes jealous of this, so that now and again Leopold had to put on performances in which she featured more prominently.

The Mozarts left Munich for Augsburg, Leopold's birthplace, so he could proudly display his child prodigies to his former fellow citizens. Here they also met the famous piano builder, Johann Andreas Stein, from whom they purchased a "pianoforte" which from then on became part of their permanent baggage. In Mozart's time the pianoforte (also known in its first form as the "Hammerklavier") slowly began to supersede the harpsichord because on the pianoforte the intensity of the sound could be varied (in Italian "piano" and "forte" mean "soft" and "loud"). By the end of the 18th century, the pianoforte had evolved into our modern grand piano.

After giving concerts in various German cities, the Mozart family arrived in Frankfurt am Main on August 12, 1793, more than two months after they had left Salzburg. Leopold made the following announcement in the local press: "...During the concert the girl of twelve and the boy of seven will perform. Both will play the harpsichord or pianoforte... and the boy will also perform a violin concerto... The keys of the pianoforte will be covered with a cloth and the boy will still play perfectly, as if he could see them... moreover, from a distance he will recog-

View of Frankfurt (detail). Here the fourteen–year–old Goethe attended a concert given by the Mozart family.

nize all notes produced individually or as chords by the pianoforte or any other conceivable instrument, including church bells, goblets, carillons, and so on. Finally he will improvise, for as long as you wish to listen to him, in whatever key you propose to him, even the most difficult, and not only on the pianoforte but also on the organ... The price is 1 Thaler per person. Tickets are on sale at the Golden Lion Inn."

It is little wonder that almost 60 years later the German writer, Johann Wolfgang von Goethe, who attended this concert as a 14–year–old, could still conjure vividly the image of "the little dandy with his wig and his sword."

The Marchioness Pompadour, long–time mistress of Louis XV, in a youthful portrait by François Boucher. (Paris, Louvre)

After calling in on a number of other cities in Germany the family arrived in Brussels in October 1763. Neither the reigning prince, Karel van Lotharingen, nor his wife did much for them. As Leopold wrote: "...the prince hunts, stuffs himself, and drinks a lot, and does not have a penny."

They did not have much more success in Paris where they stayed from November on. They were twice invited to the court by Madame de Pompadour, and by Louis XV himself, which resulted in a few concerts.

This portrait was painted in London in 1764–65 by Johann Zoffany. The question is whether it really does represent "Mozart with a bird's nest." (Salzburg, Mozarteum)

Queen Charlotte of England in a portrait by Thomas Gainsborough (London, Victoria and Albert Museum). Mozart dedicated his Six sonatas for harpsichord and violin (opus 3) to her. These were published in London in 1765. He composed them when he was eight years old, as stated on the title page on the right.

On April 10, 1764, the Mozarts left Paris for London, where they stayed for almost one and a half years. This was one of the most difficult periods of the tour. At first they were received by King George III and his wife and received 25 guineas for each concert. But there were problems with public concerts. In those days there was a flourishing concert life in London, led by Johann Christian Bach and Karl Friedrich Abel. The season, however, had already progressed too far and not enough members of the public came to the two concerts the Mozarts organized in June. To make matters worse Leopold fell ill and had to go to Chelsea (at that time outside London) to recuperate.

Wolfgang availed himself of this opportunity to compose his first orchestral work, a symphony. Nannerl copied out the instrumental parts. They returned to the capital in the autumn, but did not give many performances. Wolfgang wrote another six sonatas for harpsichord and violin (opus 3), which he dedicated to Queen Charlotte and which were published there. He was greatly influenced by Johann Christian Bach, who had instantly recognized his genius and who instructed and stimulated him. He also attended performances of Handel's oratorios and operas in the Italian style. These experiences were of crucial importance to his later work. We know from one of Leopold's letters from this period that Wolfgang, eight years old, now wanted to write an opera...

In July 1765, Leopold decided to leave London. After a brief stay in Canterbury, the Mozart family embarked at Dover for Calais and traveled to The Hague by way of Lille, Ghent, and Rotterdam. The child prodigies were supposed to be received there by the Prince of Orange but, sadly, first Nannerl became seriously ill and then, at the beginning of November, the same happened to Wolfgang; he remained in a kind of coma for eight days.

In January the family arrived in Amsterdam, where they gave a number of concerts, interrupted by a further stay in The Hague. Finally, they departed for Paris by way of Utrecht, Rotterdam, Antwerp, Brussels, Valenciennes, and Cambrai.

The Nieuwe Kerk in Amsterdam, by Isaac Ouwater. (Amsterdam, Rijksmuseum)

Little Wolfgang Mozart playing the harpsichord during a concert organized by Prince Conti in Paris. This painting by Michel Barthélémy Ollivier dates from 1766. (Paris, Louvre)

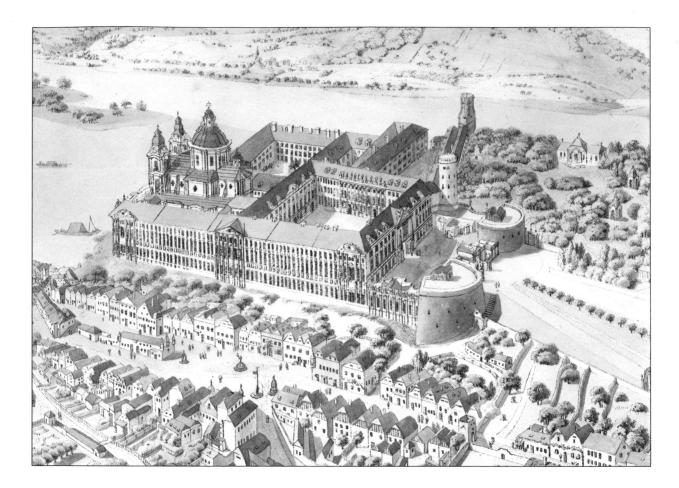

On May 10, 1766, they arrived in the French capital and stayed there until July 9 of that same year. They were not able to give many concerts, but they were received again at court. There they were given a letter of introduction to the famous writer, Voltaire, whom they intended to visit during their journey home. Unfortunately, Voltaire was ill and could not receive them. However, they did give a concert in Lausanne for the Prince of Württemberg. They traveled to Munich by way of various Swiss cities, including Berne and Zurich. In Munich they were again received by Elector Maximilian III. During the midday meal he gave Wolfgang a theme, consisting of four bars, on which he had to improvise.

By the end of November 1766 the Mozarts were back home again in Salzburg. Leopold had remained away much longer than his leave allowed, but the archbishop did not make too much of a fuss; after all, the Mozarts had helped spread the fame of the Salzburg court. Leopold got back his job as vice–Kapellmeister. Moreover, during their trip he had managed to save quite a bit of money.

Wolfgang had made so much progress during the tour that he was now, 11 years old, appointed court concertmaster and received several commissions for compositions. In two months he composed the musical comedy *Apollo and Hyacinthus*, which was performed on May 13, 1767.

Leopold thought the climate in Salzburg too provincial for his child prodigies, however, and decided to go to Vienna, where they arrived in September after a journey of 8 or 9 days along the Danube. They made a few stops on the way to give concerts; at the Abbey of Melk, for example, where Wolfgang played the organ.

Above: *View of the Danube, close to Vienna. (Vienna, Museen der Stadt)*
Left: *Dr. Anton Mesmer, pioneer of "animal magnetism," who commissioned the Singspiel,* Bastien and Bastienne *from Mozart.*

Above left: *The Abbey of Melk, where Mozart played the organ while on the way to Vienna. (18th–century print, Vienna, Museen der Stadt).*

The atmosphere at the court in Vienna had changed since their first stay. Franz I had died and Maria Theresa now reigned, together with her son Joseph. Less money was being spent on art and entertainment. Furthermore, a smallpox epidemic broke out and this also struck the Imperial family. Leopold wanted to remain in Vienna with an eye to the coming marriage of Archduchess Marie Caroline and Ferdinand von Bourbon, King of Naples. When the family eventually fled to nearby Olmütz, it was too late – Wolfgang and Nannerl had become infected. By the end of December they had sufficiently recovered for the Mozarts to return to Vienna where they were received by the court on January 19, 1786. In a letter Leopold complained that this had yielded nothing, at least not any money.

Wolfgang composed the opera *La Finta semplice* on commission. This was based on a text by the famous Italian dramatist, Goldoni. Despite the many eulogies this opera received from music lovers and theater personalities it was never performed, much to the anger of Leopold, who had also heard from Salzburg that the archbishop would no longer pay his stipend while they were touring.

Luckily, the Emperor and Dr. Anton Mesmer now stepped in to help, both of them giving Wolfgang a commission. Mesmer taught at Vienna University and was well–known for his theories on "animal magnetism." ("Mesmerism" can be regarded as one of the predecessors of modern hypnotherapy.) He wanted a *Singspiel* (an opera in which the text is alternatively spoken and sung) based on the tale of *Bastien and Bastienne*, a French love story. The work was performed in Mesmer's house or garden on October 1, 1768. Then, the Emperor desired Wolfgang to compose a mass for the inauguration of a new orphanage. This *Missa Solemnis*, *KV 139* was performed on December 7, 1768, in the presence of the court. The papers spoke of an "important occasion."

View of Verona, with its famous arena, which is still used for operatic performances. (Vienna, Museen der Stadt)

Right: Mozart was not only a virtuoso on the harpsichord, the piano and the organ, but also on the violin, which he started playing at an early age.

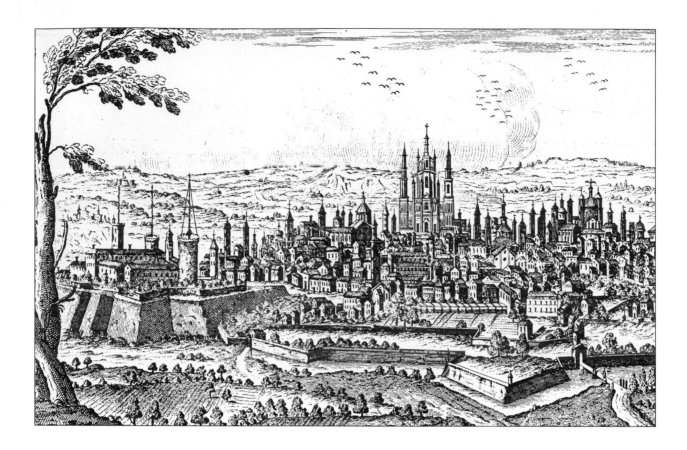

Milan in an engraving dating from
1770. (Milan, Civica Raccolta
Stampa Bertarelli)

Leopold now decided to return to Salzburg, where the family arrived on January 5, 1769. This journey had been extremely important for Wolfgang's musical education; he had heard operas by Gluck, Hasse, and Piccinni, so extending his knowledge of the musical theater. Moreover, he had been able to listen to concertos and chamber music by Joseph Haydn, Ditters von Dittersdorf, Boccherini, and Florian Gassmann, the court Kapellmeister.

In the year of the Mozarts' stay in Salzburg, Wolfgang learned Latin and read a great deal. On May 1, 1769, the archbishop finally allowed a performance of *La Finta semplice*. Wolfgang also composed the mass *Pater Dominicus, K 66*, which was performed on October 15th.

Leopold now considered that a journey to Italy would be of great importance to Wolfgang's further education. Father and son departed on December 10th or 11th, while mother and daughter remained in Salzburg. Nannerl rarely left the city of her birth again and became a well–known and much–esteemed music teacher.

Leopold and Wolfgang traveled through Tirol towards the Brenner Pass. They gave concerts in Innsbruck, Bolzano, Trento, and Rovereto, After this they stayed for 15 days in Verona, where reports of highly successful concerts appeared in the paper. On January 23, 1770, after a stop in Mantua, they arrived in Milan where they were received by the Governor of Lombardy, Karl von Firmian, a brother of the Archbishop of Salzburg.

Wolfgang gave a concert in the Governor's palace in the presence of numerous members of the aristocracy and the city's most famous musicians, including Giovanni Battista Sammartini, who, according to tradition, embraced the child prodigy after the concert. Mozart had composed four arias based on texts by Metastasio for the occasion. Many concerts then followed, with similar success.

Wolfgang corresponded with his sister and his mother from the start of the Italian journey, and his letters were lively and witty. From Milan he wrote: "Talking about little pigs, here you have one: I am well, praise and thank the Lord, and I wait impatiently for a reply. I kiss Mamma's hand and I pinch my sister so hard that she'll get a blister as if she had the chicken pox..."

Now Wolfgang was commissioned by Governor von Firmian to compose an opera for the 1770 Christmas celebrations in Milan. Leopold planned to travel further in the meantime, first to Rome, where they wanted to spend Easter, and then to Naples. After signing the contract for the opera, they left Milan for Lodi and Parma. In all probability Wolfgang composed one of his first string quartets in Lodi, and in Parma he met the famous singer, Lucrezia Aguiari.

A page from the manuscript of Mozart's first string quartet (in G major, K 80), composed in Lodi at seven o'clock in the evening on March 15, 1770 (Berlin, Staatsbibliothek).

The next stop was Bologna, home of Padre Giambattista Martini, the greatest contemporary expert in counterpoint (the technique of writing music in polyphonic style.) He paid Wolfgang the honor of attending one of his public concerts.

In Florence, Wolfgang met the most important friend of his youth, the English violinist Thomas Linley, who only lived to be 22. They made music together for two days.

The Mozarts arrived in Rome by way of Sienna, Orvieto, and Viterbo, just in time for Holy Week. On April 12th, they attended a church service in St. Peter's where Wolfgang met the influential Cardinal Pallavicini, among other people.

The famous anecdote concerning the *Miserere* by the composer Allegri originated during this stay in Rome. The *Miserere* was the property of the Sistine Chapel, and it could not be performed anywhere elsc, nor could the score be published. Wolfgang listened with all his concentration to this far from simple polyphonic work, returned home and at one sitting wrote down the music from memory. At the second performance he had the score with him so that he could check it.

From Rome Wolfgang continued to write his amusing letters home: "I am, thank God, in good health, me and my poor pen! ... I kiss my mother's hand, and also the nose, the neck, the mouth and the face of my sister and, oh what a naughty pen I have!, also her bottom, as long as it is clean..."

The Mozarts, father and son, spent May and June in Naples. The fact that they were Austrian nationals also stood them in good stead in the Kingdom of the Two Sicilies – the Queen of Naples was Maria Carolina, Archduchess of Austria, who well remembered the little Wolfgang and received him warmly. Leopold was fascinated by the beauty of the city, but its inhabitants he considered to be rough and uncivilized, much like Londoners. Wolfgang reaped his customary success.

After a visit to Pompeii and Herculaneum, the Mozarts once again set off for Rome. Leopold noted: "The idea of having to leave Naples saddens me, because of the beauty, the fertility, the vitality and very many more wonderful things. But when I think of the filth, the multitude of beggars, the loathsome, yes, even heathen people, the bad education of the young and the deprivation found even in the churches, then it lightens the burden of leaving this beautiful place."

On the way to Rome the coach in which they were traveling was involved in an accident and Leopold injured his leg. After a journey of 26 hours they finally reached the Eternal City, where a pleasant surprise was awaiting them. Cardinal Pallavicini had arranged that on July 8th Pope Clement XIV would bestow the insignia of the Order of the Golden Spur on Wolfgang. This honor had earlier been bestowed upon the famous composer, Gluck. Wolfgang never used the accompanying title "cavaliere" (knight), however.

Leopold and Wolfgang now traveled north and reached Bologna by way of Civita Castellana, Loreto, Pesaro, Forlì, and Imola. In Bologna, pleasant surprises were again awaiting Wolfgang. They were allowed to lodge in the house of Count Pallavicini Centurioni, who had a son of Wolfgang's age. Wolfgang became very

The Teatro San Carlo in Naples. Mozart attended many concerts here.

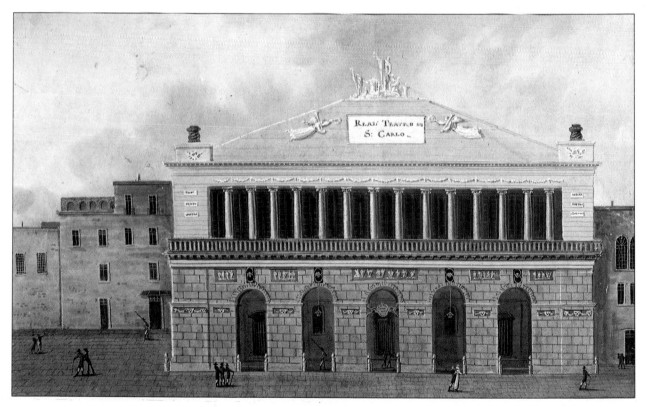

Breaking the Journey, *anonymous oil painting. (Vienna, Museen der Stadt)*

close friends with this boy, who played the harpsichord and spoke three languages. Furthermore, at the intercession of the famous music theorist, Padre Martini, Wolfgang was able to take examinations for admission as a member of the Accademia Filarmonica of Bologna. The libretto of the opera he had to write for Milan, *Mitridate, Re di Ponto*, had also arrived.

For the entrance examination Wolfgang had to appear before a ceremonial meeting of the members of the Filarmonica. He was given a theme, taken from a Gregorian chant, from which to make an arrangement for four voices. To the surprise of the members he only required half an hour for this task, rather than the customary three hours...

Left: *Pope Clement XIV, who appointed Mozart a Knight of the Order of the Golden Spur.*

Left: *Wolfgang's entrance diploma to the Accademia Filarmonica in Bologna (Salzburg, Mozarteum)*

Below: *Title page of the opera* Mitridate, Re di Ponto.

PRINCEPS   CAETERIQUE

ACADEMICI   PHYLHARMONICI.

Omnibus, et fingulis praefentes Literas lecturis, felicitatem.

Uamvi ipfa Virtus fibi, fuifque Sectatoribus gloriofum comparet Nomen, attamen pro majori ejufdem majeftate publicam in notitiam decuit propagari. Hinc eft, quod hujufce noftrae PHYLHARMONICAE ACADEMIAE exiftimationi, & incremento contulere, fingulorumque Academicorum Scientiam, & profectum patefacere intendentes, Testamur ... Wolfgano ... Mozart ... Salisburg ... fub die Menfis ... Anni ... inter Academiae noftrae ... adfcriptum fuiffe. Tanti igitur Coacademici virtutem, & merita perenni benevolentiae monumento profequentes, hafce Patentes, Literas fubfcriptas, noftrique Confeffus Sigillo impreffo obfignatas dedimus.

Bononiae ex noftra Refidentia die ... Menfis ... Anni ...

Princeps.

MITRIDATE
RE DI PONTO.
DRAMMA PER MUSICA
DA RAPPRESENTARSI
NEL REGIO-DUCAL TEATRO
DI MILANO
Nel Carnovale dell' Anno 1771.
DEDICATO
A SUA ALTEZZA SERENISSIMA
IL
DUCA DI MODENA
REGGIO, MIRANDOLA ec. ec.
AMMINISTRATORE,
E CAPITANO GENERALE
DELLA LOMBARDIA AUSTRIACA
ec. ec.

IN MILANO, MDCCLXX.
Nella Stamperia di Giovanni Montani.
CON LICENZA DE' SUPERIORI

The Palazzo della Mercanzia in Bologna. (Venice, Biblioteca Nazionale Marciana)

Leopold and Wolfgang stayed three months in Bologna. During the course of the tour Wolfgang had grown and was proud of the fact that he had been tanned by the Italian summer sun. His letters bear witness to his sharp powers of observation and his cheerful nature. He wrote to the Cardinal Pallavicini as follows: "We have the honor of meeting regularly here a certain Dominican. Everyone regards him as a saint. I do not altogether agree with this. As breakfast he often takes a cup of chocolate, followed by a large glass of Spanish wine. I myself have had the honor of dining with this holy man. During the meal he drank a good deal of wine, and finished with an enormous glass of liqueur; he ate two large pieces of melon, peaches and pears; he drank five cups of coffee one after the other, a plate of cloves and two full plates of curds. Perhaps all this was necessary for his diet, but I do not believe it, it is too much; moreover he also eats a great deal in the afternoon."

In the latter part of his stay in Bologna Wolfgang had lessons every day from Padre Martini and worked on the opera *Mitridate, Re di Ponto*. Before he left, the padre presented him with the first two volumes of his own *History of Music*.

Portrait of Padre Martini, the music theorist, from whom Mozart had lessons in Bologna. (Bologna, Civico MuseoMusicale)

View of the Riva degli Schiavoni in Venice. (Venice, Biblioteca Nazionale Marciana)

Leopold and Wolfgang left Bologna and arrived in Milan, by way of Parma and Piacenza, on October 18, 1770. Wolfgang put the finishing touches to the recitatives of the opera, waited for the soloists and then wrote the arias, especially adapted to the singers' abilities. The premiere of *Mitridate, Re di Ponto* took place on December 26th and was a great success. From behind the harpsichord Wolfgang himself conducted three performances, one after the other, which lasted a total of six hours (including three ballet–intermezzi). In a letter to his wife Leopold described in detail how the performances had been received, boasting that every aria had been greeted by the public with cries of "Viva il Maestrino, viva il Maestrino!" An impressario immediately offered Wolfgang a contract for a new opera, to be performed during the 1772–1773 season.

After their triumphs in Milan, the Mozarts stayed for a fortnight or so in Turin. In February 1771 they left for Venice, where they were promptly introduced into aristocratic and intellectual circles. Leopold, however, began to make himself increasingly unpopular because at every turn he saw intrigues against Wolfgang. The German opera composer, Johann Hasse, wrote to a friend: "Considering his age, the young Mozart is absolutely a child prodigy and I am mad about him. But his father, as far as I am acquainted with him, is always and everlastingly dissatisfied... He adores his son but seems to do things that will harm him rather than the opposite. But I believe so strongly in the natural genius of the boy that I hope he will not allow himself to be spoilt by the adoration of his father and that he will become an honest man!"

A page of the manuscript of Ascanio in Alba, "Serenata teatrale," composed by Mozart when he was 15 years old.

Leopold and Wolfgang left Venice on March 12th and arrived back in Salzburg, by way of Padua, on March 28th. Awaiting them was the good news that from Vienna Empress Maria Theresa had commissioned a "Serenata teatrale" for the occasion of the marriage of her son, Archduke Ferdinand, to Maria Beatrice D'Este, which was to take place on October 15th of that same year in Milan.

Wolfgang worked until August on this commission, which was the opera *Ascanio in Alba*. Furthermore, he composed another three symphonies and three church sonatas, while at the same time studying the music of his contemporaries, particularly that of Joseph Haydn. In August, he went with his father to Milan where the fifteen–year–old's opera was premiered on October 17th, with the collaboration of, among others, the famous castrato, Manzuoli, who was a friend of the Mozart family. Its success completely overshadowed an opera by Johann Hasse, performed during the same period. This angered Empress Maria Theresa, who took lessons from the old Hasse. In a letter to her son, the recently–married Archduke, she advised against taking Wolfgang into his service, something which Leopold had pressed for. Greatly disappointed, the Mozarts returned to Salzburg.

The last image Wolfgang had of Milan was horrifying: "I kiss my mother's hand. Greetings to all friends. I saw them hang four villains in the Cathedral Square. They do that here, just like they do in Lyon."

Leopold and Wolfgang arrived back in Salzburg on December 16, 1771, on the exact day that Prince–Archbishop Sigismund von Schrattenbach died. He was succeeded by Hieronymus von Colloredo (1732–1812), who had strong links with the court in Vienna. He was a man of progressive ideas but had an authoritarian character. German musical tradition interested him less than Italian music and he appointed an Italian to the post of Kapellmeister. Leopold remained vice–Kapellmeister. Wolfgang, who was still court concertmaster, now received a hundred and fifty florins a year. He wrote the opera *Il sogno di Scipione* for the inauguration of the archbishop on April 29, 1772.

On October 24, 1772, Leopold and Wolfgang left for the third and last time for Italy. In Milan, Wolfgang, in collaboration with the singers, had to write the arias for the new opera *Lucio Silla*. The opera was due to be premiered in January 1773. Wolfgang wrote to his sister about it, saying that he hoped her thoughts would be with him during rehearsals. He closed his letter with the usual jokes: "...have you heard what happened here? I'll tell you. Today we left Count Firmian's palace to go home and when we got to our street we opened the door of our house, and what do you think happened? We went inside!

Goodbye, my lung; I kiss you, my liver and remain as always, my stomach, your worthless frater brother Wolfgang. I implore you, I beseech you, my sister, tickle me, scratch me." Unfortunately, the performances of *Lucio Silla* were much less successful than those of *Ascanio in Alba* had been the previous year. Leopold wanted Wolfgang to enter the service of Archduke Leopold, Grand Duke of Tuscany, but the archduke refused point blank. Subsequently, Leopold decided to return home and they arrived back in Salzburg in March 1773.

This last Italian trip marked the end of an important phase of Wolfgang's life. He was no longer a child prodigy, but an adolescent, and he was also at the threshold of adulthood as a composer.

In the years 1773 to 1777, the Mozarts' difficulties with Archbishop Colloredo, who would no longer permit them to tour, began in earnest. In July 1773, when the archbishop was away for a while on his travels, the Mozarts left for Vienna. They stayed there for two months, in the vain hope that Wolfgang might be appointed Kapellmeister to the court. Letters home were now written in secret code so that no one would discover Leopold's plans for his son, should the letters fall into the wrong hands. Wolfgang made a joke of this when he signed a letter to his sister: 'Oidda. Gnagflow Trazom. Niew, red 12 tsugua 3771'. (It is only necessary to read the words backwards...)

Impression of Vienna in the 18th century, a painting by Franz Scheyerer. (Vienna, Museen der Stadt)

Archbishop Colloredo, who was called "the Mufti" behind his back, could not refuse the Mozarts permission to travel to Munich, where Wolfgang was to conduct his opera, *La Finta giardiniera*, at the carnival in January 1775. To have done so would have offended Elector Maximilian III. Apart from this, however, Colloredo remained implacable on the question of touring, a stance which would eventually lead to conflict.

During their short stay in Vienna, Dr. Franz Anton Mesmer again organized a concert in which Wolfgang performed. Like many scholars of his time, Mesmer was a freemason. He was not so much interested in the mysterious and esoteric aspect of the rituals as in the propagation of progressive political and social ideas. A fellow lodge member, Baron Tobias Philipp von Gebler, who later became Grand Master of the important Viennese Lodge of the Grand Alliance, had written a heroic drama for which Wolfgang composed the music – *Thamos, re d'Egitto*. The musical drama was a tribute to freemasonry and its origins, which could be traced back to the priestly caste in Ancient Egypt. It was Wolfgang's first important acquaintance with freemasonry, an acquaintance which would lead to membership and be crowned with the composition of the opera *Die Zauberflöte (The Magic Flute)*.

In Salzburg, Archbishop Colloredo commissioned Wolfgang to write an opera, *Il Re pastore*, which was performed on April 23, 1775, in honor of the visit of Archduke Maximilian Franz, the Elector of Cologne. But in September of that same year Colloredo closed the theater in Salzburg so that the inhabitants,

The 21-year-old Mozart with the decorations of the Golden Spur. (Bologna, Civico Museo Musicale)

who loved their musical theater very much, could no longer attend performances. For Wolfgang this was the last straw; he saw his chances of furthering his career in Salzburg by means of his operas evaporating. He resigned himself to this until 1777 and composed music for the court orchestra, the moneyed classes, and the church.

Left: Anna Maria Pertl, Mozart's mother, portrayed in 1775. (Attributed to Pietro Antonio Lorenzoni, Salzburg, Mozarteum.) She probably did not play an instrument. She died in Paris at 54 years of age.

In March 1777, Leopold wrote to the archbishop requesting that he and Wolfgang be allowed to undertake a journey. There was no answer. A second request was denied by Colloredo. To a third request he answered that Wolfgang was quite old enough to travel without his father. Leopold concurred with this and decided that his mother, Anna Maria, would accompany Wolfgang. Colloredo continued to make difficulties and on August 1, 1777, Wolfgang himself submitted an extremely polite request. After 28 days, the archbishop reacted by dismissing both Leopold and Wolfgang. His ironic answer was: "Father and son are given permission, as the Gospels teach us, to try their luck elsewhere."

View of the center of Munich in the 18th century.

Leopold managed to have his dismissal rescinded but on September 23, 1777, Wolfgang and his mother left for Paris by way of Munich, Augsburg, and Mannheim. With mixed feelings Leopold and Nannerl stayed behind in Salzburg, but Wolfgang was deliriously happy. In Munich he saw various *Singspiel* performances and decided enthusiastically to write opera in this genre. His later works *Die Entführung aus dem Serail* and *Die Zauberflöte* are examples of this.

In Augsburg, his father's birthplace, Wolfgang was much impressed with his cousin Maria Anna Thekla, nicknamed "das Bäsle." "She is beautiful, intelligent, pleasant, sensible and jolly ... It is true that we also get on together because she is rather mischievous. We tease people together. What fun we have!", he wrote of her. Once she and Wolfgang sang a canon together in honor of a friendly abbot. But to his cousin's great delight, instead of the written text he softly sang dirty words.

Wolfgang took his leave of Augsburg with an extremely successful concert. Mother and son left for Mannheim, which at that time was an important center of music and art. This was thanks to the Elector of the Palts, Karl Theodor, who on the death of Maximilian III on December 30, 1777, also became Elector of Bavaria.

Wolfgang did not manage to enter his service, but the friendly treatment he received from his colleagues persuaded him to stay until March 1778.

Leopold Mozart was deeply disappointed that Wolfgang did not become Kapellmeister in Mannheim and in a letter he reproached him angrily for his frivolity, something which, indeed, echoed through Wolfgang's letters. These letters show on the one hand the self–assurance of an adult while on the other they are full of adolescent jokes about "shit, shitting, arse kissing, in thought and word, but not in deed," as he wrote to his father. Furthermore, Wolfgang fell in love with a lovely girl, Aloysia Weber, who had a wonderful voice. She was his first great love, the sister of his later wife, and he was never able to forget her. To Leopold's fury he

Anna Maria Thekla, Mozart's cousin, who was two years younger than he and nicknamed "das Bäsle," in a portrait painted in 1778. (Salzburg, Mozarteum)

The national theater in Mannheim in a lithograph by J.B. and J.S. Klauber.

The singer Aloysia Weber – here in theatrical costume in an engraving by Johann Esaias Nilson (Salzburg, Mozarteum) – was Mozart's first great love. He fell in love with her during a journey they made together at the end of January, beginning of February 1778, from Mannheim to Kirchheim–Poland. There they were received by Princess Caroline van Oranje Nassau–Weilburg, a sister of Stadtholder Willem V of the Netherlands, and gave a concert. Mozart wanted to tour Italy with the 17–year–old, but his father forbade it. A year later, Aloysia refused his marriage proposal. He finally married her sister, Constanze.

View of Paris from the Pont Royal, *by Charles Laurent Grevenbroeck.*

therefore remained in Mannheim instead of going to Paris. He wanted to go to Italy with Aloysia, but Leopold forbade him. He reconciled himself to the situation and on March 14th he departed for Paris with his mother, dejected because he had to leave Aloysia behind.

In Paris he came into contact with Jean Le Gros, organizer of the famous "Concerts spirituels." He wrote two symphonies and the well–known *Concerto for flute, harp and orchestra, KV 299,* among other things, for him. He moved in masonic circles and met Otto von Gemmingen, an important man in Austrian freemasonry, whose lodge "Zur Wohltätigkeit" in Vienna he would later join.

But in Paris things did not turn out as he would have liked, and his mother noticed this too. The aristocracy behaved arrogantly, refused

Left. A page from the manuscript
of the Paris Symphony of 1778.
(Salzburg, Mozarteum)
Above: A 17th–century lithograph
of a Paris salon. (Paris,
Bibliothèque des Arts Décoratifs)

him admittance or talked during his concerts. Wolfgang conceived a deep aversion for the Parisians whom he found "ugly and ill–mannered in musical affairs."

After the business failure came the tragedy of Anna Maria Mozart–Pertl's death, probably from a form of typhus. She first became ill in the middle of June 1778, but she refused to allow French doctors to examine her. At 10 o'clock on the evening of July 3, 1778, she breathed her last. A few hours later Wolfgang wrote a letter to Leopold in which he only warned him that Anna Maria was seriously ill. The true bad news was given to a family friend in Salzburg, Abbot Bullinger, who had to tell Leopold. Finally, on July 9, he himself wrote to his father to tell him what had happened.

Wolfgang found himself in a remarkable situation. Despite his grief at his mother's death, he also felt a weight had been lifted from his shoulders. His thoughts were increasingly with Aloysia and the Weber family, with whom he had continued to correspond. Leopold wanted him to find a position in Paris, but Friedrich Melchior Grimm, secretary to the Duke of Orléans and an old friend of the family, who

The Mozart family in an oil painting by Johann Nepomuk Della Croce (Salzburg, Mozarteum), with the mother, Anna Maria, seen in a portrait on the wall.

had helped them during their previous visit in 1763, was now less positive. In a cynical, hypocritical letter to Leopold he wrote, among other things: "...he (Wolfgang) is too honest, not active enough, too easy to cheat, not eager enough for opportunities of success. To be successful here you must be enterprising and spirited. For his own good I wish he had half his talent and twice as much spirit of enterprise... I wish I could help him."

For various reasons, however, Grimm wanted to be rid of the Mozarts. At the time there was a foolish conflict going on between the composers Gluck and Piccinni. Grimm supported the latter while Wolfgang sided with the much more gifted Gluck.

Although Wolfgang was beginning to achieve some success at the "Concerts spirituels," he could not withstand the pressure of Grimm and his father. On September 28, 1778, he left Paris, arriving in Salzburg in January 1779. He made various unforeseen stops and the journey took three months – a form of protest against his father, who still considered him incapable of tackling life alone. Wolfgang wanted to prove the opposite, but he also wanted to go to Munich to see Aloysia Weber again. She had joined Elector Karl Theodor's theater, and had quickly turned into a prima donna who no longer wanted anything to do with a "second-rate" musician from Salzburg. In the meantime, oddly enough, he had written a letter, full of erotic innuendo, to his cousin Maria Anna Thekla, inviting her to Munich (did he have a premonition?). As a form of comfort, she accompanied him home to Salzburg, back to the yoke of his father Leopold and Archbishop Colloredo.

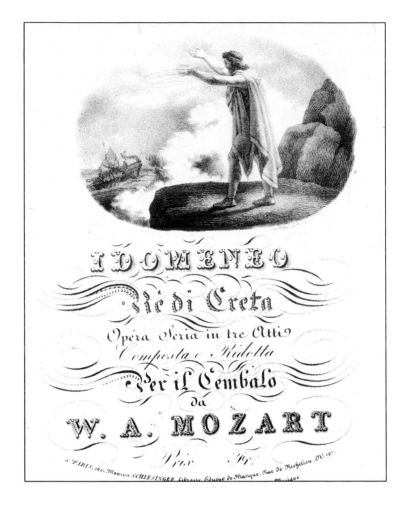

Indeed, he was immediately forced to petition the hated Colloredo in order to obtain the post of organist (at the paltry remuneration of 450 florins a year), which his father had gotten for him. In the two years that Wolfgang remained in Salzburg – which he found deadly dull – he wrote symphonies and short works. The row with his father continued to smoulder; his sister, Nannerl, had become an old spinster, the type of woman he loathed. Happily, important musical figures, including Emmanuel Schikaneder (1751–1812), the future librettist of *Die Zauberflöte*, visited the city.

In October 1780, Wolfgang's great chance came along. The new Elector of Bavaria, Karl Theodor, commissioned him to write an *opera seria* for the occasion of the 1781 carnival in Munich. This was a great honor because "serious" opera was held in higher regard than *opera buffa* (light opera), for which he had been earlier commissioned in Milan.

With much difficulty Wolfgang obtained six weeks leave from Archbishop Colloredo so that he could go to Munich to work on his new opera, *Idomeneo, Re di Creta*. Despite the death of Empress Maria Theresa on November 29, 1780, the carnival inMunich went ahead. Colloredo had departed for Vienna to pay tribute to the new Emperor, Joseph II, and so Leopold and Nannerl were able to go to Munich for the premiere. It was a huge success. Before Wolfgang threw himself into the carnival festivi-

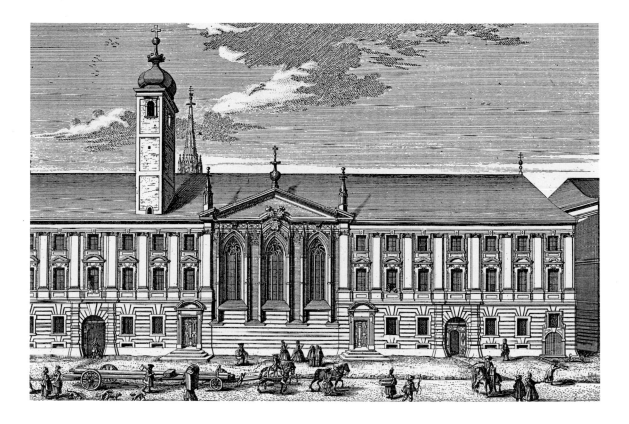

The "German House" in Vienna, where Archbishop Colloredo lodged, and from where Mozart was literally kicked out of his service.

ties, he composed the *Quartet for oboe and strings, K 370*, a serenade, and a *Kyrie* for the Elector.

Wolfgang had planned to return to Salzburg, but Archbishop Colloredo summoned him to Vienna, where he arrived on March 16, 1781. He was received with extreme coolness at the palace and was forced to eat with the cooks. The orders were that he could not participate in the musical life of Vienna, unless something was organized by the Salzburg court. Wolfgang was furious and sought the support of his old friend, Dr. Mesmer. The first conflict with Colloredo soon arose when a charitable society for widows and orphans asked Wolfgang to collaborate on a concert. Colloredo could not refuse this request, but when the concert turned out to be a success he ordered Wolfgang to leave within a few days. Now Wolfgang put into action a plan which he must have thought out beforehand. He knew that in Vienna he could easily earn the paltry annual salary which he received in Salzburg by giving private lessons and concerts. He defied the archbishop, left the palace, and moved in with Cecilie Weber, Aloysia's mother, who rented rooms. Aloysia was married to the actor, Joseph Lange. Her singing career had made her rich, and she supported her mother financially. On May 9th, Mozart had to appear before the archbishop. In a letter to his father Wolfgang described the course of the conversation: "These were his first words: 'Well, when is the young man leaving?' – 'I wanted to leave tonight, but there was no place.' Then he exploded and said in one breath that I was the worst scoundrel he knew, that nobody served him as badly as I did and that he advised me to leave immediately, or he would order my honorarium to be stopped."

The poster for the concert of April 3, 1781, in Vienna. One of Mozart's symphonies (perhaps that in C major, K 338) was performed and he himself played the piano-forte.

Wolfgang took not the slightest notice of this and in June, after much bickering, he offered his resignation through Count Arco, the famous *chef de cuisine* of the court. This was refused, and the count literally kicked him out of the palace. After this he wanted nothing more to do with Salzburg and the court and although he had not actually been dismissed he now regard-

Above: *Mozart's wife, Constanze Weber.*
Above right: *The marriage certificate, dated August 4, 1782.*

ed himself as a free man. Wolfgang was a rebel at heart, and it is not difficult to see why he was so interested in freemasonry, which was progressive and supported the ideals of the French Revolution.

How did Wolfgang live those first months in Vienna? He wrote to his father and described how he spent his day: "In all the seasons I am coiffed at six o'clock and fully dressed by seven. I write until nine o'clock. From nine to one I give lessons. Then lunch, unless I am invited somewhere, then it is two or three o'clock... it is impossible to work before five or six in the evening, and then I often have another concert. Otherwise I write until nine o'clock. Then I go to my beloved Constanze, where the pleasure of seeing her is spoilt by the sour behavior of her mother... if necessary I write again until one o'clock, if I come home early..."

The "beloved Constanze" was Constanze Weber, the sister of Aloysia, who had rejected Wolfgang. Constanze was therefore something of a second choice, but love certainly played a role in their relationship. Despite the objections of Leopold and Nannerl, the couple were married on August 4, 1782, in St. Stephan's Cathedral in Vienna. Constanze was certainly not the perfect housewife. She spent money freely and loved to flirt. Nor did she fully understand that she was married to a genius. She did not inhibit Wolfgang, however, and shared a difficult life with him without too much quarrelling, although she often adopted an independent attitude.

Mozart had competitors in Vienna – naturally. (By now, when the name "Mozart" was mentioned everyone thought of Wolfgang Amadeus and no longer of Leopold...). One of them was the greatest pianist of his time, Muzio Clementi, with whom he was friends. There was little love lost, however, between Mozart and Salieri. Antonio Salieri was court composer and extremely proud of his successes in France. Mozart, however, was convinced of his own superiority in the dramaturgical field, though he was jealous of Salieri's facility in musical affairs and in his association with the aristocracy. Despite this rivalry, however, there is no reason to attach any truth to the story that Salieri poisoned Mozart out of jealously.

Nannerl, Mozart's sister, about 30 years old. (Salzburg, Mozarteum)

Antonio Salieri, court composer,
and Mozart's great rival in Vienna.

Six Sonates
Pour le Clavecin, ou Pianoforte avec
l'accompagnement d'un Violon
Dediés
A Mademoiselle
IOSEPHE D'AURNHAMER
par
WOLFG. AMADEE MOZART
Oeuvre 2.
Publieset se vendent chez Artaria Compl
a Vienne.

Mozart did not write much during the early months of his stay in Vienna, his new place of residence. He only composed the major *Serenade, K 375*, the *Sonata for 2 pianos, K 448* and a series of sonatas for violin and harpsichord (or piano) which were published by Artaria in 1781 and highly praised in the trade press (K 376, 377, 379, and 380). Another *Kyrie* and various sonatas for wind instruments date from the same year. But Mozart was giving much more thought to the opera which he had already planned when he was in Mannheim. This was to be a *Singspiel*, suitable for the Burgtheater in Vienna, which had been opened in 1778 specially for German operas. The theaters artistic director, Gottlob Stephanie, a freemason, suggested *Belmonte and Constanze or the Abduction from the Harem* for the libretto. The project was meant to have been complet-ed for the arrival in Vienna of Archduke Paul of Russia, the son of Catherine II, in the autumn of 1781. It was not finished, however, and the premiere took place on July 16, 1782.

By this time Mozart had formed definitive ideas about the composition of operas. As he wrote to his father on October 13, 1781: "It is absolutely necessary that the poetry is the obedient child of the music." Although *Die Entführung aus dem Serail*, as the opera finally became known in German, was well attended after a lackluster premiere, Mozart earned little more than a part of the receipts. Copyright did not exist at that time and publishers could print scores without paying the composer a penny. After the premiere the Emperor spoke the historic words: "Too many notes, my dear Mozart;" to which Mozart gave the equally historic answer: "Sire, not one more than necessary!" Too many notes or not, the whole of Germany would become acquainted with Mozart's first true operatic masterpiece.

After the premiere of *Die Entführing*, in the period just before his marriage, Mozart devoted himself once more to instrumental music. He composed serenades, the string quartets which are dedicated to Haydn and three piano concertos, K 413, 414, and 415. With his piano concertos Mozart had chanced upon a new source of income. He was able to organize "academies": subscription concerts which took place in all the major cities throughout the entire century. The musician acted as his own impressario, rented or borrowed a suitable place from friends – this could be a palace or a room in a café – made known how many academies would take place, and took subscriptions. In 1783, Mozart did extremely well in this way. He earned 1,000 florins, a sum which he had probably never before seen all at one time.

Gottlob Stephanie, artistic director of the Burgtheater in Vienna, and one of Mozart's patrons (Vienna, Museen der Stadt)

In the academies Mozart performed alone as a pianist, or with others. He was also obliged to compose new music for this purpose. Sometimes he composed works for friends, such as the hornplayer Ignaz Leitgeb, from Salzburg. Leitgeb had planned to turn his back on music and had started a cheese business in Vienna with money borrowed from Leopold Mozart. The business was unsuccessful and he was forced to start playing again – so he could pay Leopold his money back, for one thing. Mozart wrote four horn concertos for him – but not without pulling his leg, sometimes on the original scores: "Adagio for you, Mr. Donkey – Animo – presto – cheer up, oh how flat – oh what a bloody bore!," and so on. Sometimes the poor Ignaz was forced to pick the sheets up off the floor or to wait until the music was completed.

"Wolfgang Amadé Mozart has taken pity on Leitgeb, donkey, fool and featherbrain. Vienna, May 27, 1783.' These words on the title page of a concerto for the hornplayer express the cheerfulness of this period of Mozart's life.

In the summer of 1783, Mozart was busy with two operatic projects. *The Goose of Cairo* was a libretto by Abbot Varesco of Salzburg, who had also written the libretto for *Idomeneo*. *The Deceived Bridegroom* was a libretto by Lorenzo da Ponte, whom Mozart had just met.

Decor design and mise–en–scène for Die Entführung aus dem Serail *by Johann Christian Schöller. (Vienna, Museum der Stadt)*

Da Ponte was an Italian Jew who was actually called Emanuele Conegliano and who came from Ceneda in the Veneto region. He was born in 1749 and was half adventurer, half man of letters. In order to be able to study he had become an abbot and after 1,001 adventures in Vienna ended up as a protegé of Salieri. He would later provide the librettos for *Don Giovanni, The Marriage of Figaro,* and *Così fan tutte.* He died in the United States in 1838. In his memoirs of 1823, he talks about a certain Mozzart (sic) that he became acquainted with after 1783, but from Mozart's letters it appears that their first meeting actually took place in 1783. The project he was presently engaged on with Da Ponte did not go ahead, nor did that with Varesco. Only the incomplete scores of both operas exist.

On June 17, 1783, Constanze and Wolfgang's first child was born. He was named Raimund, although Mozart had promised his father to name him Leopold. The name was chosen by a friend, the Baroness Wetzlar, and Wolfgang did not dare to oppose her. In his own inimitable way he found a compromise by writing to his father that the boy was actually called Raimund Leopold, and therefore actually only Leopold...

In an attempt to effect a reconciliation with his father, Wolfgang and Constanze traveled to Salzburg so that Leopold and Nannerl could meet Constanze for the first time – after first making sure that Archbishop Colloredo would not throw Wolfgang into jail. The visit was not a success. Constanze did not find favor with either Leopold or Nannerl. (After Wolfgang's death, sister and sister-in-law both lived in Salzburg, but they never called on each other.)

On August 19, 1783, news reached Salzburg that little Raimund had died. This was nothing unusual at a time when infant mortality was extremely high, but it was a great blow to the Mozarts. Later, back again in Vienna, Mozart still spoke about his "big, fat little man." They took their leave of Nannerl, who a short time later married a village dignitary from the minor aristocracy in Sankt Gilgen, older than she and a widower with five children. They journeyed back to Vienna along the Danube, stopping on the way at Linz, among other places. Mozart gave a concert there on November 4th. He had quickly completed a symphony, the *Linz Symphony, K 425*, for the occasion.

Above: *Lorenzo da Ponte, the librettist, in an engraving by Michele Pekenino.*

Right: *Mozart accompanying the soprano Caterina Cavalieri (ps. of Franziska Cavalier). (Vienna, Museen der Stadt)*

*View of Linz, where the Mozarts
stayed with Count
Thun–Hohenstein, and where
Mozart performed the* Linz
Symphony.

Vienna in Mozart's time.

1784 and 1785 were the happiest years of Mozart's life. He had plenty of work, his creativity had reached its peak, and he was famous both as a composer and as a pianist. He bought two notebooks. In one he kept his household accounts and in the other he noted his compositions, as soon as they were completed. These were piano concertos, a piano quintet, and sonatas for various instruments. A sonata for pianoforte was dedicated to Thérèse von Trattnern, in whose house the Mozarts had lived for a short time. It is not clear whether there was more than friendship between her and Mozart. Letters from this period are missing and were probably destroyed by Constanze.

In 1784, Mozart met the famous Neopolitan opera composer, Giovanni Paisiello, with whom he became good friends. On September 21, 1784, the Mozarts' second child, Karl Thomas, was born. He became a government civil servant and lived until 1858. At the end of 1784, Mozart completed the quartets which are dedicated to Haydn, but the most important event of

that year was probably his admission into the "Zur Wohltätigkeit" masonic lodge on December 14th.

The initiation of a blindfolded candidate in the masonic lodge "Zur gekrönten Hoffnung" around 1786. In all probability, Mozart is the first on the right, with a "Freundschaftsmasche" (friendship noose).

The singer Nancy Storace. Mozart thought her fascinating.

Mozart was a great advocate of freemasonry and also made his friend and teacher, Joseph Haydn, a member, as well as his father, Leopold. On April 20, 1785, Mozart conducted the cantata *Die Maurerfreude* (*The Joy of Freemasons*) at a banquet at the most important Viennese lodge, "Zur gekrönten Hoffnung." The Grand Master of this lodge, minerologist, and scientist Ignaz von Born, appears in the person of Sarastro in *Die Zauberflöte* (*The Magic Flute*).

In this period Mozart had another female friend, the singer Nancy Storace. He was fascinated by her blonde beauty and her lovely soprano voice, but again it is unclear whether they had an intimate relationship.

At the beginning of 1785, Leopold Mozart also came to Vienna to see how his son was faring. He was extremely satisfied, particularly because Mozart had 2,000 florins in the bank and was able to pay his rent of 460 florins. He now lived in a spacious first floor apartment, his umpteenth house in Vienna, but still not his last. On April 25th, Leopold again set out for Salzburg. Mozart accompanied him a few kilometers outside Vienna. He was never to see his father again.

W.A. Mozart in an 18th–century engraving. (Vienna, Museen der Stadt)

In spite of his success, Mozart was not swell–headed. Many contemporaries remarked on this. One of them, the young musician Gyrowetz, related (about himself in the third person): "Mozart appeared to be the most friendly of all the musicians who were present. He looked at Gyrowetz, who was still very young, with a sympathic gaze, as if he wanted to say: 'You're entering the big, wide world for the first time anxiously awaiting what the future will bring and what your fate will be.' This gaze touched the young Gyrowetz deeply, and from that moment on he was devoted to Mozart with all his heart." The singer, Michael Kelly, gave the following vivid portrait of Mozart: "He was a very small, extremely thin, pale man, with beau-

proud. He amiably invited me to his house; I accepted his offer, and stayed a long time." Taking courage from this friendly reception, Kelly let Mozart see a few of his compositions. Mozart had to disappoint him, and he did this in a friendly manner but without mincing his words: "Dear boy, you asked my opinion, and I shall give it to you honestly: if, when you were in Naples and still had no other profession, you had studied composition, you would probably have been successful. But now that you must devote all your attention to your career as a singer, it would be very foolish to commence on another dry study... Listen to me and don't do it."

Mozart himself was happy about the fatherly feelings Haydn entertained for him. He dedicated six quartets to him. These were published by

Below left: The title page of the six quartets dedicated to Haydn.

Below right: The dedication in Italian "al mio caro Amico Haydn."

SEI
QUARTETTI
PER DUE VIOLINI, VIOLA, E VIOLONCELLO.
Composti e Dedicati
al Signor
GIUSEPPE HAYDN
Maestro di Cappella di S. A.
il Principe d'Esterhazy & &
Dal Suo Amico
W. A. MOZART
Opera X.
In Vienna presso Artaria Comp.
Mercanti ed Editori di Stampe Musica
e Carte Geografiche.

Al mio caro Amico Haydn

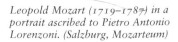

the music publisher, Artaria, in 1785. The love and admiration he had for the old master can be seen from the letter, written in Italian, in which he dedicated the quartets.

The health of Mozart's own father, Leopold, deteriorated steadily over a period of a few months and he died on May 28, 1787. His legacy was divided between his two children, who afterwards lost touch with each other almost completely.

Mozart himself only had four and a half more years to live. In a letter to his father on April 4, 1787, he had remarked: "I never go to bed at night without thinking that perhaps tomorrow I will be no more."

The announcement of the premiere of The Marriage of Figaro *on May 1, 1786, in Vienna. (Vienna, Gesellschaft der Musikfreunde)*

In the last five years of his life, Mozart busied himself with – among other things – five large–scale opera projects: *Le Nozze di Figaro* (*The Marriage of Figaro*), *Don Giovanni, Così fan tutte, Die Zauberflöte* (*The Magic Flute*), and *La Clemenza di Tito*.

The first three were Italian operas because after 1783 there was a preference for these in Vienna. Returns from German opera in the Burgtheater had fallen, despite the success of Mozart's own *Die Entführung aus dem Serail*.

Mozart himself had suggested to librettist Lorenzo da Ponte that he use Beaumarchais' play as a the starting point for *Figaro*, though he knew that this comedy had been banned by the Emperor because of its daring content. In the play, master (Count Almaviva) and servant (Figaro), were treated as equals and, further-more, the intrigues and the hypocrisy of the aristocracy were ridiculed. It is not difficult, however, to understand Mozart's preference for the piece, considering the echoes of the ideals of freemasonry and the French Revolution which resound through it.

Da Ponte managed to persuade the Emperor – who was very interested in a new work by Mozart – that the opera would offend nobody. So Mozart went to work in the summer of 1785 and completed the opera in the spring of 1786. The premiere took place in the Burgtheater on May 1st in front of an enthusiastic audience. The success of the premiere did not lead to a flood of performances, however; in the whole of 1786 the opera was performed in Vienna only nine times.

Meanwhile, Mozart also composed new works, such as piano concertos, for his academ-ies, but these were less and less successful. It seemed as if the Viennese public was beginning to turn its back on him and because of this Mozart's income fell steadily. He and Constanze did not cut their coats according to their cloth, however, and so began a period of a continual shortage of money, a problem which increasingly had to be solved by loans from friends and acquaintances.

In October 1786, the Mozarts' third child, Johann Thomas Leopold, was born, but he died

a month later from "suffocating convulsions."
At the end of that year Mozart received an invitation to go to Prague, where *Figaro* was to be
performed. When Constanze and he arrived in
Prague in January 1787, the whole city talked of
nothing else. Mozart's academies, in which he
improvised on themes from the opera, were an
enormous success. This eased the financial problems to some extent. The opera saved the
Italian company which was performing it from
bankruptcy and it commissioned a new opera
from Mozart, with a libretto of his own choice.

In February 1787, the couple returned to
Vienna, promising to return to Prague in the
autumn. In spring Mozart probably had a few
meetings with the sixteen–year–old Beethoven
who had come to play for him with the aim of
becoming his pupil. According to one of
Mozart's biographers, he remarked about
Beethoven that "people will hear a great deal of
that young man." Beethoven, however, was

*View of the city of Prague, with
the famous Charles' bridge in the
center.*

A group of musicians accompanying the bridal procession. An 18th–century design by Moritz von Schwind for the opera The Marriage of Figaro.

Left: 19th–century theater costumes for a performance of The Marriage of Figaro. (Vienna, Museen der Stadt)

forced to return to Bonn because his mother was dying and he never saw Mozart again.

This time the librettist Da Ponte made the suggestion for the subject of the new opera: *Il dissoluto punito ossia il D. Giovanni, dramma giocoso in due atti* ("Licentiousness punished or Don Giovanni, a cheerful drama in two acts"). Neither the music nor the libretto were finished when Mozart and Constanze returned to Prague in October. They went to stay with friends in the Villa Bertramka (now the Mozart Museum), where Mozart put the finishing touches to the opera. In all probability the great Don Juan and seducer of women, Giacomo Casanova, who was a friend of both Da Ponte and Mozart and who was staying in Prague at the time, helped to make the last improvements to the libretto. Perhaps he even contributed part of the role of the servant, Leporello.

The overture was still not completed the evening before the premiere. While Mozart composed, Constanze had to prepare punch and tell him stories. That cheered him up, but the punch made him sleepy. He wanted to lie down and asked Constanze to wake him up in an hour. He was sleeping so soundly, however, that Constanze let him sleep until 5 o'clock in the morning. Still, when the copyist arrived at seven the score was ready and the opera was premiered on October 29, 1787.

View of the citadel of Prague, in Mozart's time the capital of Bohemia. (Vienna, Museen der Stadt)

Don Giovanni was much less successful with the public than *The Marriage of Figaro*, but it did provide the opera company and Mozart with a reasonable amount of money. The Mozarts left Prague in November, after Mozart had written another aria – *Bella mia fiamma, K 528* – for Josepha Duschek, who had been his hostess in the Villa Bertramka.

When Mozart arrived home in Vienna there was both a pleasant and an unpleasant surprise awaiting him. After the death of the composer Gluck on November 15th the Emperor had appointed Mozart court composer. But instead of the honorarium of 2,000 florins which Gluck had received, Mozart was awarded only 800 florins.

On December 27th, the Mozarts' fourth child, a daughter they named Theresia, was born. She died in June the following year, also of "intestinal convulsions."

When *Don Giovanni* was premiered on May 7, 1778, in the National–Hoftheater in Vienna, the Emperor had criticisms: "The opera is heavenly; it is perhaps even more beautiful than Figaro, but it is not something my Viennese can get their teeth into." When librettist Da Ponte reported the Emperor's words to Mozart, he is said to have answered: "Let's give them time to chew on it..."

The opera was a success for a long time in Vienna, but the inhabitants of the city, nonetheless, soon seemed to forget Mozart once again. In 1788, the last three great symphonies were created, among them the *"Jupiter" Symphony*, in addition to chamber music (the *Clarinet quintet, K 581*) and music for the court. The Second Turkish War led to economies in Viennese cultural life and did nothing to improve Mozart's financial situation.

In April 1789, Mozart traveled to Germany with Count Lichnowsky, one of his patrons and also his pupil, in the hope of being able to augment his income. It was the first time he had been separated from Constanze and he wrote her several loving and witty letters. The two travelers first went to Prague, where the ambiance was no longer the same for Mozart as it had been during his operatic successes, and then tra-

The church and school of St. Thomas in Leipzig, where J.S. Bach was Cantor. His successor was visited by Mozart (Leipzig, Bach Museum).

Right: The singer Henriette Baranius (Mozart's mistress?) in a lithograph by Friedrich Bolt.

veled on to Dresden. Here Mozart earned a tobacco box full of coins for a concert at the court. In the days that followed there was a sort of competition between various musicians in organ and piano playing which Mozart won without the slightest difficulty. From Dresden Mozart wrote to Constanze: "Dear little wife, I have a number of requests of you: 1. I request you not to be melancholy 2. to look after your health and to distrust the spring weather 3. not to go out alone on foot, better still, not to go out on foot at all 4. to trust in my love. I never write you a letter without having your portrait before me 5. I request you to attend to your behavior, not only because of your honor and mine, but also for the outside world. Do not be angry at this request. You must love me even more because I value my honor... Oh Stru! Oh Stri! I kiss you and hug you 1095060437082 times."

From Dresden, they went to Leipzig where Mozart visited Johann Friedrich Doles, the successor to J.S. Bach as Cantor of St. Thomas' Church. He also attended a concert there and examined Bach manuscripts. Via Potsdam, Berlin, and Dresden again, the two travelers returned to Leipzig where Mozart had a row with his companion. He was forced to pay back money he had borrowed from Lichnowsky, at which Lichnowsky departed, leaving Mozart

behind, penniless. Fortunately, he was helped by Cantor Doles. He now decided to go first to Berlin again in order to attend performances of *Die Entführung aus dem Serail*. There are indications that in this period he had an affair with the singer Henrietta Baranius, with whom he rehearsed the role of Blondchen for his opera.

Leopold II, Grand Duke of Tuscany, succeeded his brother, Joseph II, as Emperor of Austria in 1790, and dismissed many musicians and theater people linked to the Viennese court, including Antonio Salieri and Lorenzo da Ponte.

On June 4, 1789, Mozart was back in Vienna. Circumstances were bad. Constanze was very ill and he had run out of money. Constanze went to the health spa at Baden to recuperate. When she returned, she gave birth to their fifth child, Anna Maria, who died an hour later.

One bright spot during this difficult time was a commission from Emperor Joseph II to write a new opera. This was *Così fan tutte* ("All women are the same"), an opera buffa, with a libretto by Da Ponte. It appeared that the tale of two girls who deceive their fiancés had been passed on by the Emperor and had really happened. The premiere took place on January 26, 1790, before a fairly enthusiastic audience.

Mozart's financial worries continued to plague him, and he asked the new Emperor, Leopold II, for an appointment as second court Kapellmeister. He received no answer, nor was he invited to the coronation on October 9, 1790, in Frankfurt am Main. This was probably because he was a freemason and consequently, in the eyes of the new emperor, a supporter of the French Revolution. And despite the fact that during the festivities his own *Piano Concerto No. 19, K 459*, together with the *Piano Concerto No. 26, K 537*, later named the "Coronation Concerto," were probably performed.

In the nine years that Wolfgang and Constanze Mozart were married six children were born. Only two survived: on the left Franz Xaver Wolfgang (July 26, 1791 – July 29, 1844), musician; on the right is Karl Thomas (September 21, 1784 – October 31, 1858), government official, in an oil painting by Hans Hansen.

A reconstruction of the Mozart family's last house in Vienna, in Rauhensteingasse. Their apartment was on the first floor.
Below: The title page and the first page of the libretto of La Clemenza di Tito, *which the poet Caterino Mazzolà had based on Pietro Metastasio's play of the same name.*

LA CLEMENZA
DI TITO,
DRAMMA SERIO PER MUSICA
IN DUE ATTI
DA RAPPRESENTARSI
NEL TEATRO NAZIONÁLE
DI PRAGA
NEL SETTEMBRE 1791.
IN OCCASIONE DI SOLLENIZZARE
IL GIORNO DELL' INCORONAZIONE
DI SUA
MAESTA L'IMPERATORE
LEOPOLDO II.

NELLA STAMPERIA DI NOB. DE SCHÖNFELD.

INTERLOCUTORI.

Tito Vespasiano, Imperator di Roma.
Vitellia, Figlia dell' Imperatore Vitellio.
Servilia, Sorella di Sesto, amante d'Annio.
Sesto, Amico di Tito, amante di Vitellia.
Annio, Amico di Sesto, amante di Servilia.
Publio, Prefetto del Pretorio,

La Scena è in Roma.

La musica è tutta nuova, composta dal celebre Sig. Wolfgango Amadeo Mozart, maestro di capella in attuale servizio di sua Maestà imperiale.

Le tre prime Decorazioni sono d'invenzione del Sig. Pietro Travaglia, all' attual servizio di S. A. il Principe Esterazi.

La quarta Decorazione è del Sig. Preisig di Coblenz. Il vestiario tutto nuovo di ricca e vaga invenzione del Sig. Cherubino Babbini di Mantova.

Mazzola

74

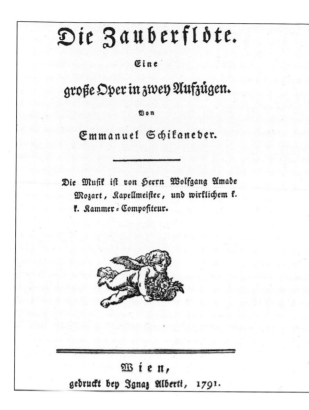

Constanze's health remained poor in these years, and she took the waters regularly in Baden, where Mozart occasionally visited her. In September 1790, he decided to go to Frankfurt for the coronation, with or without an invitation, and sold furniture and cutlery in order to pay for the journey. In Frankfurt he gave an academy, but without much success. Then he traveled to Munich, by way of Mainz and Mannheim. There he met many old friends and gave a concert in honor of the King of Naples, who was visiting Munich. Back in Vienna, it seemed that no one wanted him, not as a composer, not as a teacher, not as a performing musician. He decided to concentrate on the only task that he had at court – composing dance music. An invitation from the Italian Opera Company reached him from London, but he could not accept it due to lack of money.

In the first months of the last year of Mozart's life, 1791, he created various works, including the *Piano Concerto in B–flat major, K 595*. This was the last in a series of piano concertos which

Mozart had developed to a level that perhaps only Beethoven reached later.

The idea for the opera *Die Zauberflöte* (*The Magic Flute*) came to Mozart in the spring when an old acquaintance, the librettist Emmanuel Schikaneder – who was also short of money – suggested they should write an opera together. The work was completed in July and was premiered on September 30th in the Freihaus–Theater auf der Wieden, with Mozart as conductor. It was an enormous success and many performances followed, some of which Mozart also conducted. Mozart worked many of the ideas of freemasonry into this opera, particularly ideals stemming from the Enlightenment concerning educating man into high–principled beings by means of wisdom, love, and goodness. According to very recent Dutch research, ideas and symbols derived from classical alchemy also play a role in the opera.

While he was still working on *Die Zauberflöte*, he received a commission from Prague to present another opera, *La Clemenza di Tito*, on the occasion of the festivities there for the coronation of Leopold II. Mozart wrote this opera in six weeks and stayed in Prague with Constanze from the middle of August until the middle of September. On September 6th, he himself conducted the premiere, in the presence of Emperor Leopold II and his consort.

In July of that year Constanze had returned from Baden and on July 26th she gave birth to their sixth child, Franz Xavier Wolfgang. In his turn he became a musician and composer, shamelessly advertising himself everywhere as the "son of Wolfgang Amadeus," and sometimes signing his compositions with his father's name. He died in Karlsbad in 1844.

Decor and mise–en–scène for the first act of Die Zauberflöte (The Magic Flute) *by Joseph and Peter Schaffer (Vienna, Museen der Stadt). From left to right:* Tamino, Queen Astrifiammante's the three ladies–in–waiting and Papageno.

In the meantime, Mozart had received a request from a secret patron (probably Count Walsegg) to write a *Requiem*. He worked on this during October and November 1791, the last two months of his life. In October he went once again to Baden to visit Constanze and in November he conducted his *Kleine Freimaurer–Cantata* at the dedication of the new temple of his masonic lodge "Zur gekrönten Hoffnung." His health, meanwhile, had greatly deteriorated and from November 20th on he was bedridden.

Had he lived, his financial troubles would have been over, because at the beginning of December members of the Hungarian nobility offered an annual honorarium of 1,000 florins.

Just before his death, Mozart conducted a rehearsal of the Requiem *from his sickbed.*

On December 4th, a rehearsal of the still uncompleted *Requiem* was held at his bedside.

The night after, December 5, 1791, at one o'clock in the morning, Wolfgang Amadeus Mozart died. He was 35 years old.

The burial was simple. No cross was placed on his grave so that later his resting place could no longer be determined.

Constanze kept secret the fact that Mozart's pupil, Franz Xaver Süssmayer, completed the *Requiem*, so that she would be able to collect

Biographie
W. A. Mozart's.

Nach Originalbriefen, Sammlungen alles über ihn
Geschriebenen, mit vielen neuen Beylagen,
Steindrücken, Musikblättern und einem
Fac-simile.

Von

Georg Nikolaus von Nissen,
Königl. Dänischem wirklichen Etatsrath und Ritter vom Dannebrog-
Orden etc. etc.

Nach dessen Tode herausgegeben

von

Constanze, Wittwe von Nissen,
früher Wittwe Mozart.

Mit einem Vorworte vom *Dr. Feuerstein* in Pirna.

Leipzig, 1828.
Gedruckt und in Commission bey Breitkopf und Härtel.

the honorarium from Count Walsegg. She asked
the Emperor for a small pension, which she received. She let rooms in her house and in so doing
met a Danish diplomat, Georg Nikolaus von
Nissen, whom she married and went to live with
in Copenhagen.

In 1820, von Nissen's greatest wish was ful-
filled; he was able to settle in Salzburg with
Constanze and write Mozart's biography. This
was published posthumously in Leipzig in 1828.
Mozart's sister, Nannerl, ill, blind, and bitter,
continued to live in Salzburg until she died in
1829. Constanze took in her sisters, Aloysia and
Sophie. She died in 1842 and was buried beside
father Leopold.

Above left: *Constanze Mozart in a
portrait by Hans Hansen painted
in 1802. (Salzburg, Mozarteum)*
Above right: *Title page of the first
edition of Mozart's biography by
Georg von Nissen (in the portrait).*

The Most Important Works of Wolfgang Amadeus Mozart

Operas	*Die Entführung aus dem Serail, K 384*
	Le Nozze di Figaro (The Marriage of Figaro), K 492
	Don Giovanni, K 527
	Così fan tutte, K 588
	Die Zauberflöte (The Magic Flute), K 620
	La Clemenza di Tito, K 621
Choral Works	*Krönungsmesse (Coronation Mass) in C major, K 317*
	Requiem in D minor, K 626
Symphonies	*No. 31 in D major, K 297, "Paris"*
	No. 35 in D major, K 385, "Haffner"
	No. 36 in C major, K 425, "Linz"
	No. 38 in D major, K 504, "Prague"
	No. 40 in G minor, K 550
	No. 41 in C major, K 551, "Jupiter"
Piano Concertos	*No. 20 in D minor, K 466*
	No. 21 in C major, K 467
	No. 23 in A major, K 488

Violin Concertos	*No. 26 in D major, K 537 "Coronation Concerto"*
	No. 3 in G major, K 216
	No. 4 in D major, K 218
	No. 5 in A major, K 219

Violin Concertos

No. 26 in D major, K 537 "Coronation Concerto"

No. 3 in G major, K 216

No. 4 in D major, K 218

No. 5 in A major, K 219

Horn Concertos

No. 2 in E–flat major, K 417

No. 3 in E–flat major, K 447

No. 5 in E–flat major, K 495

Other Concertos

For flute and harp in C major, K 299

For clarinet in A major, K 622

Symphony concertante for violin, viola, and orchestra in E–flat major, K 364

Chamber music

"Haffner" Serenade, K 250

Serenade for wind instruments and double bass, K 361, "Gran Partita"

String Quartet No. 17 in B–flat Major, K 548, "Hunt"

String Quartet No. 18 in A major, K 464

String Quartet No. 19 in C major, K 465, "Dissonant"

Clarinet Quintet in A major, K 581

Serenade in G major, K 525, "Eine Kleine Nachtmusik"

Motet "Ave verum corpus" in D major, K 618